The Catholic Church in Oregon and the Work of Its Archbishops

BOOKS BY JOHN R. LAIDLAW

*The Catholic Church in Oregon and the
Work of Its Archbishops*

*These Things I Remembered and Poured Out
My Soul in Me*

The Catholic Church in Oregon and the Work of Its Archbishops

John R. Laidlaw

An Exposition-Testament Book

Exposition Press   *Smithtown, New York*

First Edition

© 1977, 1980 by John R. Laidlaw

"The Oldest Bishop: Archbishop Edward D. Howard" and "The Return of Archbishop Dwyer" are reprinted from *These Things I Remembered and Poured Out My Soul in Me,* by John R. Laidlaw.

Library of Congress Catalog Card Number: 80-66196

ISBN 0-682-49608-1

Printed in the United States of America

To the Most Reverend Cornelius M. Power, D.D., J.C.D.,
Archbishop of Portland in Oregon,
with deep respect and gratitude

Contents

Preface

The short book of essays known as *These Things I Remembered and Poured Out My Soul in Me* has met such a kind reception that I feel it possible to attempt another collection with special emphasis on the archbishops who have served in the Archdiocese of Portland in Oregon.

This period was marked by considerable growth of the Catholic Church in Oregon, which, at the same time, withstood grave opposition, particularly from the American Protective Association (APA) at the turn of the century, the Ku Klux Klan (KKK) shortly after the close of World War I, and the Oregon Compulsory School Bill of 1922.

During the missionary period (1838-1883), the principal opposition came after the Whitman Massacre, when H. H. Spalding, whose life had been saved by a Catholic missionary, Father J. B. Brouillet, slanderously attacked the Catholic Church, thereby stirring up some anti-Catholic feeling. The spirited defense of Father Brouillet by his many supporters, and studies of the church's action by competent scholars, however, largely alleviated the anti-Catholic feeling for the time being.

Strong political and social anti-Catholic pressures again became formidable in the 1920s. But, as before, strong defenses were mounted by the church's supporters. Aided by the influx of excellent Catholic people who sought refuge from the privations and hardships caused by the depression and the great dust bowls in the Midwest, the Catholic Church in Oregon was able to overcome her difficulties, and the period was marked by a tremendous growth and strengthening of the Catholic Church.

x   *Preface*

This growth owed much to the able guidance of the three archbishops who administered the archdiocese during these fifty-some
years.

First was Archbishop Charles Seghers (1838-1886), the
last great missionary, although he was only archbishop of this
archdiocese for a short time, returning to Victoria, B.C., at his
own request to continue his missionary labors until he was
murdered in Alaska by a crazed companion.

Second was the archbishop from Baltimore, William Gross,
CSsR, the only archbishop of this archdiocese to have been an
order priest. He succeeded Archbishop Seghers in 1883 and continued his able administration until death in 1898.

Fourth was Archbishop Alexander Christie, who served from
1900 until his death in 1925 and who led the defense against the
APA in 1900, the Oregon Compulsory School Bill in 1922, and
the many attacks made by the KKK.

Archbishop Edward D. Howard became archbishop in 1926
and continued until his resignation in 1966. He was succeeded by
Archbishop Robert J. Dwyer in 1967, who served until his resignation in 1974. Archbishop Cornelius M. Power came in April
17, 1974, our present archbishop. As a result of his request for
additional help, he has been granted two auxiliary bishops: Bishop
Paul Waldschmidt, C.S.C., and Bishop Kenneth Steiner.

The Catholic Church in Oregon and the Work of Its Archbishops

Let us now praise men of renown and of their fathers in their generation.

—Sirach 44:1

1

Archbishop F. N. Blanchet

As a result of the War of 1812 between Great Britain and the United States, in the peace treaty between the two countries, it was agreed that the Northwest country would be held under "joint occupancy" until a permanent boundary should be established. Therefore the area between the Spanish boundary on the south and the Russian territory to the north from the summit of the Rocky Mountains to the Pacific Ocean on the west should be open to both countries. The citizens of both countries should be free to engage in all lawful activities. This became particularly true of the fur trade for both. The British were engaged in the work of the Hudson's Bay Company. The Hudson's Bay and the Northwest Company had been united to each other after many savage feuds by a settlement in 1820. There were a number of French Canadians who had settled down in the area now known as St. Paul, Oregon. These were without priests or missionaries. Many had married native Indian wives and had developed families. Since they were Catholics without the solace of their faith, they asked Bishop Provencher, who had been placed in charge of the Red River country, to secure missionaries who might be sent by the Hudson's Bay transportation to the Northwest country. At first the authorities of the Hudson's Bay Company would not agree to help since they felt that the area south of the Columbia River would eventually be given to the Americans. Finally, the company agreed to help if the missionaries so transported would

1

not labor south of the Columbia River. When this was made clear, the Archbishop of Quebec, upon the recommendation of Bishop Provencher, arranged to secure two missionaries who would be satisfactory to undertake the task. In charge was placed Father Francis Norbert Blanchet.

Father Blanchet was born in 1795, the son of Pierre and Rosalie Blanchet, at St. Pierre, Rivier du Sud, and baptized September 4 in the Church of St. Francis. He attended the parish school of St. Pierre where he received his first Holy Communion and later was confirmed. In 1810 he was enrolled in the Minor Seminary of Quebec and later in the Superior Seminary from which he was ordained priest after an admirable theological course on July 19, 1819. After service of some months in the Cathedral of Quebec, he volunteered to care for the Acadians in New Brunswick. There he showed great promise in his care for the people and the sick of that difficult region. His devotion and care as a missionary priest gave him a splendid reputation, knowledge, and zeal and helped in his later care for distant Oregon. Later, Father Blanchet was made pastor of the Parish of the "Cedars" in 1827 which was under the Diocese of Montreal. There he came to know the voyageurs and Indians such as would be found in the Northwest. When the question arose of sending a priest to the Columbia country, it was decided by Bishop Provencher and the Dioceses of Montreal and Quebec to place Father Blanchet in charge of the mission to be sent by the Hudson's Bay canoes to the district of the Columbia. With him was sent Father Modeste Demers, who had shown himself glad to undertake the missionary work.

On May 3, 1838, they set out for the distant Columbia country. The journey would take six long months. The work was handled by trained and experienced voyageurs. Long stretches were covered by water in light or heavy canoes. Other sections were traversed by land on horseback. The brigade was under the command of John Rowland, a chief factor, who was a Catholic himself and very sympathetic. The travel party consisted of eleven boats laden with merchandise and included a large number of men, women, and children. They traveled between "forts" designated by names such as "Fort Constant," "Fort Cumberland," "Fort Carleton," and "Jasper House," "Norway House," etc. There were also included a number of guests such as scientists. Sad to say, a number of travelers lost their lives when twelve out of twenty-six in two boats capsized. After this terrible tragedy, the journey finally continued on into the Columbia River country down the river to Fort Walla Walla. There Peter Pambrun, who was a Catholic, received the missionaries gladly, and they were able to meet and talk with the Indian tribes of the district, who showed great interest in them and a strong desire for future missionary care. Father Demers reported, "To make fervent Christians of them, it would suffice to teach them the Christian doctrine. Nothing more is needed." From Fort Walla Walla the journey brought them to Fort Vancouver safely and happily to the end of the long trip. There they were greeted by a great crowd of white and Indian people. Since at the time the chief factor, Dr. John McLoughlin, was away in London, James Douglas in his place greeted them most cordially and arranged to help them in every way possible. Also, representatives of the French Canadians who had sought so earnestly for priests to begin the missionary work met them.

Although it had been understood that the work would not be undertaken below the Columbia River, it was hoped that Dr. McLoughlin would secure permission to work also below the Columbia where a much larger group had been established. The first mass was celebrated on November 25, 1838. The census taken at this time indicated seventy-six Canadian and Iroquois Catholics and an Indian population estimated at three hundred. Not too long afterward, Dr. McLoughlin returned with the welcome tidings that the Hudson's Bay authorities had removed the former ban against the activities below the Columbia River line.

The largest settlement was established at St. Paul. A log chapel had been built by the French Canadian settlers in preparation for the missionaries. This was visited and approved but at the suggestion of Dr. McLoughlin, the log cabin was moved from its former location to a new place close to the present permanent church. Father Blanchet also asked for a land grant to supply necessary property for a permanent church, rectory and property for schools, and a residence for sisters.

In the meantime, after the mass at Fort Vancouver, every effort was made to receive those married to French Canadian Catholics whose marriages were then validated, and the children were baptized and instructed in the faith. Afterward the missionaries made visits to the Indian tribes and arranged for their instruction. For this purpose, Father Blanchet had developed the "Catholic Ladder" used by the Indians themselves under directions from Father Blanchet. Meanwhile, it was evident that more priests must be found and added to the numbers available. Some were gradually secured from Canada. Also the Jesuits had arrived as missionaries from the United States and had established missions among the Flathead tribes. A great success was accomplished by the Jesuit missionaries in Montana. During this same period, the efforts of Father Blanchet and Father Demers had made much progress in Oregon and Washington, including Oregon City and the Cowlitz country north of the Columbia River. This had caused Sir George Simpson of the Hudson's Bay Company to ask and obtain additional missionary help from Canada by way of the Hudson's Bay canoes from Canada.

Realizing the need of working with the missionaries, Father De Smet visited Father Blanchet and Father Demers at Vancouver. In the meantime, two other missionaries had come from Canada to help the others already laboring in the area. Father De Smet offered to go to Europe and by giving lectures about the growth of the church in the Oregon country to obtain priests and sisters to help in needed missionary work. It was also hoped to have church authorities appointed to assist in the growth of the Oregon country. When these facts were made known to the authorities in Rome, a vicariate apostolic with the title of Philadelphia was developed by Father De Smet, who secured an additional land claim at St. Paul, where schools and residences were established, including a school for boys and one for girls. For four years he labored, going from settlement to settlement, facing peril of a wild country, recalling the scattered faithful to the practice of religion. Two other priests from Canada came to his assistance, Reverend A. Langlois and Reverend Z. Baldas. In 1844, Father Pierre-Jean De Smet, S.J., came with four other Jesuits, three lay brothers, and six sisters of Notre Dame de Namur. Elected by Pope Gregory XVI to the titular see of Philadelphia in Lydia, December 1, 1843, and appointed vicar apostolic of Oregon Territory, Archbishop Blanchet was transferred to the titular see of Adrasus on May 7, 1844, in order to avoid confusion with the see of Philadelphia in Pennsylvania. The letters from Rome did not reach him until November 4, 1844. To receive episcopal consecration, Archbishop Blanchet started for Canada on December 5, boarded a steamer on the Columbia River, touched at Honolulu, rounded Cape Horn, landed at Deal, England, went by rail to Liverpool, took a vessel to Boston, and thence proceeded by rail to Montreal, a journey of twenty-two thousand miles. He was consecrated July 25, 1845, in St. James Cathedral, Montreal, Canada, by Bishop Ignace Bourget of Montreal, assisted by Bishop Michael Power of Toronto. After his consecration, he proceeded to Rome, where he explained to the Pope the position of the Territory of Oregon. In view of the rapid development and settlement of Oregon, Pope Pius IX resolved to erect an archepiscopal see with suffragans dioceses. Archbishop Blanchet was elected to the newly established see of Oregon City July 24, 1846. He also visited France, Belgium, Germany, and Austria in the interests of his archdiocese. He sailed from Brest, France, February 22, 1847, with five secular priests, three Jesuits, and seven sisters of Notre Dame. They reached the Columbia River on August 13, 1847. He took possession of his see on August 26, 1847, at the Church of St. John, Oregon City, on the Willamette. Father Blanchet had decided to go to Europe and Canada to be consecrated bishop and to secure funds. Later, after his return to the parish, Bishop-elect Blanchet learned that the vicariate had by a brief dated

July 24, 1846, been erected into an ecclesiastical province with three sees of Oregon City under himself as Bishop of Oregon City, and his brother, Father A. M. A. Blanchet, Bishop of Walla Walla, and Father Demers, Bishop of Vancouver Island.

Following his trip to Rome, Bishop Blanchet had made trips to various parts of Europe in the interest of the missions. As a result, he was able to bring back to Oregon large sums of money to help them and also to secure and bring back by 1847 fourteen Jesuits, four Oblate Fathers, thirteen secular priests, and thirteen sisters, and was able to start educational institutions—one for boys and one for girls.

However, the Cayuse Indians attacked the Presbyterian Mission causing the destruction of the buildings and the murder of Dr. and Mrs. Whitman and many of their followers. When certain unjust parties attempted to blame these losses upon the Catholic missionaries, considerable difficulties arose, but eventually the evidence proved conclusively that the Catholic missionaries had not only tried to prevent the attacks of the Indians but had done their best to secure the release of the captives held by the Indians after the massacre. They also had saved the life of Mr. Spalding, whom the Indians condemned to death. After the trials of the Indians, when they were in prison, Archbishop Blanchet accompanied them to the scaffold at the time of their execution.

Since so many churches and other buildings had been erected, the archdiocese was heavily in debt, and the archbishop went on a tour of many of the dioceses of South America from which he was able not only to pay the diocesan debts but to have a considerable surplus.

It was not long before Archbishop Blanchet came to the conclusion that the city of Portland, Oregon, had outgrown Oregon City to such an extent that it was necessary to change his episcopal residence to Portland for the convenience of the archdiocese. This was done.

In a letter to the cardinal prefect of propaganda, he wrote advising that his health was failing and suggested the appointment of a successor on May 23, 1862. He suggested Canada as the proper place wherein to find a new archbishop, stating that there was no one in his diocese qualified for such a position. On August 14, 1862, he issued a decree appointing Portland as his residence. He sent a letter to the cardinal prefect transferring his residence from Oregon City to Portland. On September 30, 1863, he issued a decree establishing the Church of the Immaculate Conception in Portland as the Cathedral Church.

Eventually, he was happy to welcome Archbishop Seghers as coadjutor to himself with right of succession. An injury due to a fall in a train made this particularly important. He sent Archbishop Seghers to make a long and difficult visitation of the archdiocese. Archbishop Blanchet died on June 18, 1883. At his request, he was to be buried in St. Paul, Oregon. After a solemn funeral mass in the Cathedral of Portland, his body was sent by train to St. Paul for burial. The train stopped at the cities through which it passed to enable the Catholic people to pay their respects to the first archbishop of the archdiocese who had done so much for the religion of the Northwest country. He had called the First Provincial Council of the Archdiocese of Oregon City in 1848. He had left St. Paul, Oregon, in December 1848 and taken up his residence at Oregon City. He attended the First and Second Plenary Councils of Baltimore in 1852 and 1866. In 1852, the first church in the city of Portland was dedicated under the title of the Immaculate Conception; it became the pro-cathedral when he moved his residence to Portland in 1862. He went to Canada in 1859 and took back thirty-one priests, sisters, and servants. He attended the First Vatican Council, 1869-1870, where he voted for the papal infallibility; he was still in Rome on September 26, 1870, when the temporal power of the papacy was overthrown. Infirmities began to weaken him in 1878. When Bishop Seghers was made his coadjutor in 1878, he retired to the hospital of the Sisters of Providence, Portland, Oregon. He was transferred by Pope Leo XIII to the titular archepiscopal see of Amida, December 10, 1880, and resigned his see, February 27, 1880. He administered the two districts which never had bishops. He is regarded as the "Apostle of Oregon"; due to his zealous and untiring labors, the church grew rapidly in Oregon. He died at the age of eighty-seven, June 18, 1883, Portland, Oregon. He was buried in the cemetery of St. Paul amid the oldest Canadian settlement in Oregon. His years of episcopacy: forty years; thirty-three years, seven months, and three days as Archbishop of Oregon City; sixty-four years as a priest.

2

The Second Archbishop:
Charles John Seghers

Archbishop Charles John Seghers was born in Ghent, Belgium, on December 26, 1838. A memorial tablet has been placed in the home in which he was born. He entered the University of Louvain as a deacon and was ordained a priest in Mechlin on May 30, 1863.

After ordination, Father Charles desired to work among the Indians of Northwest America. Accordingly, his superiors sent him to Bishop Demers of Victoria in Vancouver Island. Bishop Demers received him with great joy, and after some months of trial Father Seghers was incardinated, at his own request, into that diocese.

Father Seghers was soon recognized by Bishop Demers as one of his most valuable priests. He spoke English well, and his training at Louvain prepared him well to administer to the faithful in Oregon. On one or two occasions he visited Indian settlements, but his work was mostly at the cathedral in Victoria, where he showed himself invaluable. He did regret, however, that he was not able to spend more time among the Indians. "Sometimes," he wrote to his uncle in Belgium, "I sigh as I think of the abandoned condition of so many Indians and savages."

A tall, thin, young priest much beloved by the people, Father Seghers soon showed signs of tuberculosis. Bishop Demers took him to Rome as his secretary although frequent hemorrhages showed the grave state of his health. Bishop Demers was much worried about his assistant, and during a visit with Pope Pius IX, he told the Pope that he had a splendid priest but feared that he would lose him as a result of tuberculosis. Bishop Demers asked the Pope to pray for Father Seghers and to give him his blessing. The Pope did so, and Father Seghers had no more hemorrhages except one which occurred when Bishop Demers himself died.

At the death of Bishop Demers, Father Seghers was made administrator of the diocese and was appointed Bishop of Vancouver Island on March 21, 1873.

At this time, Archbishop Francis N. Blanchet of Oregon City (later Portland in Oregon) felt that he was growing old and hoped for a French-speaking, mission-minded successor. He was able to know and appreciate Bishop Seghers as the one he desired to replace him and so, at his request, Bishop Seghers was made coadjutor with right of succession to Oregon City. This was very pleasing to Bishop Seghers, and he set off to make a visitation of the archdiocese and the territory under it.

Bishop Seghers set forth on a long missionary journey to eastern and western Oregon, Idaho, and Montana. An American army officer met him camped in eastern Oregon alone. He was asked his name and identified himself as "Seghers." He was offered a ride in an ambulance which he refused and rode on horseback with the American expedition to Lakeview, Oregon.

By 1881, Archbishop Blanchet felt it best to retire, so Archbishop Seghers undertook the complete care of the Archdiocese of Oregon City. He received the Pallium on the Feast of the Assumption in 1881. The administration of the archdiocese made long missionary journeys very difficult for Archbishop Seghers. Immediately he called and presided over an Archdiocesan Synod on August 11, 1881, and a Provincial Council on August 18, 1881. He said mass and preached very frequently and worked unceasingly for the establishment of new parishes. During his time in Portland, he established St. Lawrence Parish with the appointing of a regular pastor who had the duty of building a permanent church on the west side of Portland, and he also laid the cornerstone of St. Francis Church located on the east side of Portland.

On June 18, 1883, Archbishop Blanchet died after receiving the last sacraments from Archbishop Seghers. The archbishop preached an eloquent sermon at the funeral, saying: "He was the first missionary, the Apostle of Oregon; He is to Oregon what St. Boniface was to Germany, what St. Augustine was to England, what St. Patrick was to Ireland."

In 1883, Archbishop Seghers left for Rome. There, at his suggestion, Bishop Brondel, who had been his successor as Bishop of Vancouver Island, was made Bishop of Helena, Montana. This left Vancouver Island without a bishop. Archbishop Seghers, who realized the importance of that see, particularly since Alaska had been added to it, suggested that he himself might become once again Bishop of Vancouver Island. The Pope accepted his suggestion and insisted that he still hold the rank of an archbishop. At the suggestion of Cardinal Gibbons, Archbishop William Gross was appointed to succeed him as Archbishop of Oregon City.

Elected by Pope Pius IX to the see of Vancouver Island, March 11, 1873, he was consecrated on June 29, 1873, for Victoria, British Columbia, Canada, by Archbishop Francis N. Blanchet of Oregon City, assisted by Bishop Augustin M. Blanchet of Nesqually and Bishop Louis J. d'Herbomez, O.M.I., vicar apostolic of British Columbia. His diocese comprised Vancouver Island and Alaska. A month after his consecration he left Victoria Island in July 1873, traveling by boat to this northern peninsula, touching at Sitka, then at Kodiak, a distance of 1,120 miles, and then on to Unalaska, one of the Aleutian Islands. He visited Alaska again in 1877 and made a survey of the church in that territory, evangelizing in Nulato, Ulukuk, Nuklukayet, and various points along the Yukon. He returned to Victoria via San Francisco in September 1878—for sixteen months he had been cut off from the civilized world.

He was transferred by Pope Leo XIII to the titular see of Canea, July 18, 1878, and appointed coadjutor of Oregon City and promoted to the titular archepiscopal see of Hemesa on September 28, 1878. He reached Portland, Oregon, on July 1, 1878. He undertook immediately a tour of inspection of his vast archdiocese as well as the vicariate apostolic of Idaho, at that time under the same jurisdiction. He succeeded to the metropolitan see of Oregon City on December 10, 1880. He received the Sacred Pallium on August 15, 1881. He convened a diocesan synod in August 1881 as preparation for the Second Provincial Council of Oregon City held shortly afterward. He visited Rome in 1883 in the interests of his archdiocese and in preparation for the Third Plenary Council of Baltimore. A few days after his arrival at Rome, in November 1883, he learned that Bishop Brondel of Victoria had been transferred to the see of Helena in Montana. As no titular could be found for this diocese, he generously volunteered to return to Vancouver with a view to following up his work in Alaska. His wish was granted by Pope Leo XIII, and he was back in Victoria. Archbishop Seghers turned his attention to Alaska. He felt that many opportunities for the spread of the faith both among the Indians and the white settlers awaited him. At first, he asked Father Cataldo, the Jesuit provincial, for Jesuit priests and brothers, but the reply was that he could not expect them for some time. However, to his happiness, Fathers Pascal Tosi, S.J., and Louis Robant, S.J., were assigned to him, although no brothers were available at that time.

A lay helper, Francis Fuller, had written offering his services. Francis Fuller had applied for entrance into the Jesuit order but had not been accepted. He had been employed in various capacities in different schools and missions and was a skilled hunter. Archbishop Seghers directed the Jesuit Fathers to bring him with them. The Jesuits, however, knew that Fuller had serious faults in temperament which later became very evident. With people, Fuller at first would be very friendly and cooperative, but eventually he would become most quarrelsome and difficult with those with whom he would become associated. This became evident only after spending much time with him.

When the Jesuits arrived, Archbishop Seghers began to prepare for a long and difficult journey across the mountains and along the Yukon River to a town named Nulato. He had visited Nulato before but had been called to Portland and had promised to return later.

After their arrival at Lake Lindeman and before leaving it, Archbishop Seghers, accompanied by Fathers Tosi and Robant, camped and offered the holy Sacrifice on July 30, 1886. After many difficulties and dangers, they arrived at the mouth of the Stewart River, where they found a number of prospectors, among them was one named Walker. Here the Jesuits parted from the Archbishop and Francis Fuller.

It was not long after that Fuller's disorders began to surface. Fuller had been complaining to Walker and the others—whom he had befriended—alleging dangers from the archbishop. Feeling troubled by these evident signs of mental illness, Archbishop Seghers asked Walker to go with them to Nulato, but he refused to do so. From here on it is possible to follow the events as translated:

"Strange conversation with Fuller which for this he gives proof of his insanity.

"On October 20, Brother [in his journal, the archbishop referred to Fuller as 'Brother'] sick in the evening. No wood. Had to cook supper. Fuller got up at 9:00, got supper for himself."

October 21: "The anger of Fuller at dinner; accused me of wanting to ruin him." On October 28: "Brother rose at three o'clock, made a fire, dressed and threw himself back on his bed before 5 a.m."

On November 5: "Brother says that even though he is capable of getting wood for us, he would not do it because having Indians to do it, it is not necessary that he does it." Next day: "Brother begins to take his meals after me. It is 'an idea of mine' he tells me. Brother does not get up until six o'clock."

On November 12: "Brother, who initially scorned the idea of learning Russian (the dialect spoken along the Yukon), and affects to learn Indian, accuses me of having refused to teach him Russian."

The archbishop was by then fully convinced that he was no longer safe in company with Fuller. He tried to persuade Walker or one of the others to accompany him as far as Nulato. All refused, for their sympathy was with Fuller.

Archbishop Seghers, with Fuller and three Indians, left for Nulato. On November 20, the archbishop notes, "Brother asked me how it can be that I encourage the Indians to make fun of him. For five years the Indians did the same in the Mountains. Here they are doing the same thing."

The ten-day journey to Nulato finally came to a close. On Friday evening the party camped for the last time on the bank of the frozen river. The archbishop hoped to get to Nulato for Sunday and remarked, "God be praised, it is the last day." Fuller afterward said that he thought it was the last day for him because he thought the archbishop was planning to kill him. On November 25, before bedding down for the night, the archbishop made the last entry in his journal: "Brother says that Walker predicted to him that I would give him a bad name."

Fuller wished to rest in a barrbarra for a day, but since forty miles remained, the archbishop felt it best to continue for a time until they reached Wolf Head Point, ten miles east of the entrance of the Kopuk into the Yukon. There the archbishop spread the bearskin he used as a traveling bed over one of the ledges. The Indians occupied the opposite site and Fuller slept near the archbishop. Several times during the night he paced about the fire.

Early in the morning he rose and secured his rifle from the bottom of the sled. He entered the house and busied himself with the fire and woke one of the Indians. The archbishop told him that it was too early to get up and suggested more sleep. Between six and seven o'clock, Fuller kicked the archbishop and told him to get up. The archbishop sat up and bent over to get his mittens. He was wearing a squirrelskin parka and had put an arm through one sleeve, when Fuller pointed his .44 caliber Winchester rifle at the stooping archbishop.

Archbishop Seghers was shot through the heart and died instantly. He was not yet forty-eight years old. The date was November 28, 1886.

Because of the difficulty in assembling a court, the trial of Francis Fuller did not take place until February 1888 before a judge and jury. After Walker had been called as a witness he declared that he knew of no disagreement between the archbishop and Fuller. Fuller actually stated, "It may turn out that the archbishop actually died from natural causes. I was there at the time and know what occurred."

The jury had to decide whether it was a case of murder, which would require the death penalty, or manslaughter, which would call for imprisonment. The general feeling seems to have been that it was a case of murder, but there was a great difficulty among the jurors to come to a verdict. After deliberation of many hours, the jury finally agreed on a verdict of manslaughter.

Fuller was in prison for about seven years before he was released. A story is told that some years later he was killed by a neighbor after a conflict.

The body of Archbishop Seghers was sent to Victoria, where a mortuary chapel was established off the sacristy of the cathedral. Twice I have visited the chapel where the graves of Bishop Modeste Demers, the first Bishop of Vancouver Island, Father Jonkau, the vicar general, and Archbishop Seghers are placed. At a small altar I twice said mass in the chapel.

One feels that all must be together in Heaven with the souls of many whom they served.

3

The Missionary Archbishop from Maryland: William H. Gross

When Archbishop Seghers left for his last, sad trip to the Arctic Circle, he was replaced by the zealous and cordial Archbishop William H. Gross, who had come from Savannah, Georgia.

William H. Gross was born in Baltimore, Maryland, on June 12, 1837. His father, James Gross, was of Alsatian ancestry and had fought in defense of Baltimore in the War of 1812. His mother was of an Irish family who had escaped from Ireland in the rebellion of 1798. From this background came the future archbishop's strong Catholic and American loyalties.

His schooling began at St. Vincent's parochial school, then continued at St. Charles Minor Seminary. After his graduation from college, he felt strongly drawn to the religious life and was accepted by the Redemptorist Order, which was devoted to the work of giving missions in various parishes.

On March 23, 1863, during the Civil War, Father Gross was ordained a priest. He was first stationed in the Redemptorist House in Annapolis, Maryland, where he offered himself as a chaplain in the Union Army in that area. His truly Catholic spirit as a priest of God is made strikingly clear in this story. In the vicinity of Annapolis, a savage battle was fought between the Union and the Confederate armies. During a pause for care of the wounded on both sides, the young Father Gross offered his spiritual aid to the

16

wounded and dying soldiers. Given a Union pass for that purpose joined with a warning from the commander of the dangers involved, he set forth on his mission of mercy and religion.

While caring for the Union wounded in a secluded wooded area, he met some Confederate soldiers who asked his business. At the point of their rifles, he showed them his Union Army pass and offered to help any soldiers. Quite promptly he found himself escorted with great respect to the Confederate hospital, where he cared for the wounded and dying to the best of his ability. Conducted back to the Union lines, he reported to the Union commanding officer, who praised him greatly for his courage and devotion. From that time on until the end of the war, he engaged in conducting missions in the North and South alike.

Both when in charge of mission bands and in his work as a missionary, Father Gross developed a splendid reputation as a preacher and confessor. Among his missions he conducted one in Savannah, Georgia, which was under Bishop Persico. A few years later, when giving missions in Boston, Father Gross learned that Bishop Persico had been transferred and that he himself had been named Bishop of Savannah. On April 27, 1873, William H. Gross was consecrated Bishop of Savannah. He was thirty-six years of age and had been a priest for only ten years.

Savannah had difficulties arising from conditions in the South after the Civil War. The new archbishop realized that the black people needed help, and he tried to do all he could to care for them. He arranged for hospital care and tried to help their educational needs, continuing the efforts of his predecessor, Bishop Persico.

Meanwhile, the transfer of Archbishop Seghers had left a vacancy in Oregon, and Archbishop Gross learned from Cardinal Gibbons, a good friend of his, that he had been selected for Oregon City. Cardinal Gibbons and Archbishop Ireland had realized the need for having as many native Americans as possible in charge of dioceses in order to protect the church against those who considered it something foreign and opposed to the American spirit. Thus it was thought most important to have those who were of American training and sympathy in charge of the church. This made the appointment of Archbishop Gross particularly needed in Oregon.

Archbishop Gross first arrived at the Dalles, where he found Father Alphonse Brosgeest, a Belgian priest, as pastor of St. Peter's Parish. After a brief stop, he took a boat for Portland, where he found a group of people to welcome him. His splendid reputation had preceded him: a powerful missionary much gifted as a preacher and of deep faith and piety with strong zeal for souls, he was a man to whom people were drawn.

The new archbishop soon realized there was much to do and learn in his archdiocese. At that time, the population of Oregon was ten thousand. There were twenty-five diocesan priests and four religious order priests in the whole of the archdiocese, and only two parochial schools and eight academies for girls.

Portland was developing as a widespread city in the cleft of surrounding hills and bisected from east to west by the Willamette River. The river was crossed and forded by ferries and bridges. Most of the business area was on the west side, spreading west and south of the river.

A new cathedral, 151′ × 85′, was being built on the west side, off 3rd and Stark streets, with Father John F. Fierens, a Belgian priest, as pastor. Father Fierens had been largely responsible for all of Portland and was a firm administrator who had done much for the church. He served as vicar general of the archdiocese until his death in 1893. Portland had also had another parish, dedicated to St. Lawrence, on Southwest 3rd and Sherman streets. Father Bertrand Orth was pastor.

Groups of German-speaking people, after first using St. Michael's Italian Church, needed another west side church. They were able to build a church for the German people on Southwest 15th and Couch streets, to which was later attached a school. St. Michael's then became the Italian National Church. Still occupying the original site, St. Michael's is located across from St. Mary's Academy on Southwest 4th and Mills streets. On the same block a school for boys was established under parish priests and later the Christian Brothers. Archbishop Gross had hoped to found another parish beyond St. Lawrence to be staffed by the Redemptorist Fathers. However, although priests were offered, he was unable to secure funds for this church and the project was abandoned.

On the east side, small separate towns were first beginning, especially East Portland and Albina as well as St. Johns. These would gradually be annexed to Portland proper. A deep gulch, known as Sullivans Gulch, separated the east side from Albina. The development of railroad yards to the southeast caused the growth of Albina. There a site had been donated for a Catholic Church and school by a non-Catholic named Montgomery, possibly at the urging of his wife, who had been baptized a Catholic when attending a Catholic academy. A small church was built, and a Belgian priest, Father Van Lin, became its pastor. Railroads were growing along both the east and the west banks of the river. One parish, St. Francis, served all of southwest Portland. Beyond Portland, cities were springing up in the Willamette Valley and beyond. Strong groups of immigrants were settling, especially Germans and Italians. These usually had priests of the same national antecedents supplying leadership. A good example of this was Mount Angel, some thirty miles south of Portland, where a colony of German-Swiss people established a town and a Benedictine monastery, named after the Benedictine "Engelberg" in Switzerland. A parish church and monastery were built, and in spite of a number of fires, there eventually emerged a monastery on the hill above with a college attached and a community of Benedictine nuns. A solid town with a church and school gradually developed around this religious community.

The archbishop realized that one of the great needs of the community was to care for delinquent and orphaned children. At first, a society called the St. Mary's Society of Oregon began to raise funds, but soon Archbishop Gross decided to begin a new community of nuns, known as the Sisters of St. Mary's of Oregon, whose primary work would be to care for these children. The community had first begun at Sublimity, and some young sisters, originally from Ohio, joined local sisters and began to prepare for the new work. For them, the archbishop purchased a large tract of land in the vicinity of what is now Beaverton. The property was cleared, and in spite of great hardships the group grew and established St. Mary's Home for Boys.

In 1890, my mother was engaged to my father, James Laidlaw, who at that time was British Consul and an Episcopalian. Father Fierens, in whose parish my mother lived, probably fearing that "mixed" marriages would result in loss of faith on the part of the Catholic, insisted that a marriage of such must take place only in his own rectory, not in the church proper. Needless to say, this was not agreeable to my mother, who wanted a large and beautiful wedding, and in deep distress she sought counsel from Archbishop Gross, who knew the family well from Maryland days. The archbishop replied that while he did not wish to disturb Father Fierens, he himself would go to the family home and conduct the ceremony. It was a very pleasant and attractive wedding attended by many non-Catholic friends and pioneers of early Portland. All the children were carefully reared as Catholics and kept the faith. The first three children were baptized by Archbishop Gross, but when I came in 1898, the archbishop was in Maryland where he was to die. I was baptized by Father Hughes of the cathedral and my younger sister by Archbishop Christie.

After the death of Father Fierens in 1893, Archbishop Gross assumed the care of the cathedral. This brought about a very considerable change. The area around the new cathedral had been developing as the "downtown" business district and was not so well adapted to the convenience of the people of Portland. Most of the churches had moved elsewhere, and it was felt that the property on which the cathedral stood might be converted into the site of an office building, the income of which might maintain the archdiocesan expenses.

Property was bought between Southwest 15th and 16th streets on which a new building was erected within two months to serve as a temporary cathedral. A large portion of the second floor was given over for a boys' school conducted by the Christian Brothers. The lower floor housed the temporary cathedral with a larger seating capacity than that of the old cathedral, whose windows, altar and furniture were utilized. Eventually a new and permanent cathedral would be erected on a new site with a residence for the archbishop and clergy. In the meantime, rooms were added to the rectory of the German Church to serve the archbishop and priests who staffed the pro-cathedral.

The early part of the year 1898 witnessed the celebration of the Silver Jubilee of the archbishop as a bishop. In honor of that event, a residence, situated across from the new pro-cathedral, was presented to him.

Shortly afterward, Archbishop Gross left for Baltimore. Doubtless owing to the pressure of the many events of the year 1898, his health had been seriously weakened, and shortly before he planned to return to Portland, a heart attack brought his death on November 14, 1898. His funeral mass, celebrated by his dear friend Cardinal Gibbons, was in the Baltimore Cathedral. At his request, he was buried in the Redemptorist cemetery in Baltimore.

In an administration of somewhat more than thirteen years, much real progress was made under Archbishop Gross. Some eight new churches were built in the archdiocese; and the founding of numerous parish schools has been a great service to religion.

The Benedictine Abbey and the seminary built in connection with it have given the archdiocese and other dioceses many fine priests sorely needed. The encouragement of many institutions of mercy, such as St. Vincent's Hospital, has also accomplished untold good.

The primary work of the Redemptorist Order and to which Archbishop Gross was dedicated, missions and retreats, has continued to strengthen the faith of the loyal Catholics of the archdiocese.

So it is that the work of Archbishop William H. Gross among the people of Oregon has placed an indelible mark of religion of very great value during this highly formative period in Oregon.

4

Archbishop Alexander Christie:
"In Faith and Kindness"

The sudden and unexpected death of Archbishop Gross left a large void in the Archdiocese of Oregon City. The new order of the Sisters of St. Mary's of Oregon had just begun the necessary work of caring for orphaned and dependent boys. They were afraid that their important work might not be continued. The business affairs of the archdiocese were involved, and there was much need of direction. Debts were many and they were in need of payment. In that period when the Spanish-American War had just been brought to a victorious conclusion, an archbishop who would understand and encourage the Catholic people to help the government in the necessary tasks in the Pacific Northwest was important. The new archbishop should be an inspiration who would prove to such enemies of the church as those of the American Protective Association that Catholic people were strong and loyal in support of our country.

Thus the appointment of Archbishop Alexander Christie as the new archbishop was received with great enthusiasm. He was born in High Gate, Vermont, in May of 1848, and baptized on September 3 of that year; his father, Adam Christie, was an American of Scottish descent. His mother, Mary O'Hara, was Irish and a devout member of the church. There were six boys and three girls in Alexander's family, and three of his brothers served with the Union Army in the Civil War.

When Alexander was a young boy, the family moved to Wisconsin, where there was no opportunity to attend church, although his mother did all she could to supply religious instructions to her children. Archbishop Christie later told me that he was sixteen years old when he first met a priest.

Some years later the family again moved, to Minnesota, where there were more religious opportunities. It was there that Alexander first felt called to the priesthood. When he consulted the priest of the parish about his wishes, he was advised to begin his college studies at St. John's University at Collegeville, Minnesota. His tuition was paid by the Diocese of St. Paul. At the university, he proved himself a good student and a sincere candidate for the priesthood. For his theology studies, Alexander was sent to the Grand Seminary at Montreal, finally being ordained on December 22, 1877.

After ordination, Father Christie was made pastor of the Church of the Sacred Heart at Wadeca in southern Minnesota. During a tenure of thirteen years, he proved himself a priest of great ability and zeal much beloved by the people and most successful in his operations. He was responsible for the erection of a convent, a parochial school, and an academy. It is not surprising, therefore, that the great Archbishop Ireland was much impressed by Father Christie's evident promise and used him to help him in difficult parochial situations.

Directed to found a new parish in Minneapolis, Father Christie accomplished this task with ease. Again recognizing his talents, Archbishop Ireland then transferred him to St. Stephen's Parish, which was afflicted with a large church building and had to maintain a heavy debt. Father Christie was also appointed director of the archdiocesan boys' orphanage in addition to his pastoral duties.

Father Christie's evident successes in his priestly life led eventually to his appointment as Bishop of Victoria, B.C., on June 29, 1898. Again, his talents as an administrator and builder quickly bore fruit in the establishment of an industrial school for Indian boys and the raising of many new parishes in the diocese. Not surprisingly, then, when a few months later the see of Oregon City became vacant, Archbishop Ireland's and Cardinal Gibbons's influence succeeded in having him named to fill the position.

Archbishop Christie was received with enthusiasm in Portland. He addressed a great assembly gathered to meet him with words indicating his loyalty as an American, closing with the words: "If I held the flag of the Church in one hand, I shall hold the flag of my country in the other." His words were eagerly received by the people.

The new archbishop was fifty-one years of age, handsome in appearance, and agreeable in manner. His reputation had preceded him to Oregon, and the people and clergy hoped and prayed he would help them as well. He did. Archbishop Christie at once addressed himself to the financial problems of the archdiocese, and by selling as much property to advantage as he could, he liquidated a large portion of the debts which had been incurred. He also visited each parish in the archdiocese, exhorting all to improve conditions and bring about progress.

Archbishop Christie showed great interest and activity in promoting Christian education. Growing parishes were asked to maintain elementary schools. The question of higher education also was studied with care.

The archbishop had no sooner been established in his new archdiocese than he began a period of extraordinary activity that carried him from one end of the archdiocese to the other, planning, organizing, and beginning project after project. He went down to Woodburn to arrange for the building of a church, hastened to Astoria for the same purpose, and then went all the way down to Marshfield to see what could be done for that distant area. Back at the cathedral in Portland, he arranged for the improvement of the pro-cathedral.

Then came a great opportunity for higher education which he quickly grasped. The Methodist church had secured property on the bluff overlooking the Willamette River, near the St. Johns area. An additional large tract had also been purchased for future expansion. Unfortunately, however, the Methodists had overextended themselves and the property reverted to the real estate company. Sensing a good business and educational opportunity, the archbishop bought the property and persuaded the Holy Cross Fathers of Notre Dame, Indiana, to establish a high school and college to be known as Columbia University. Father E. P. Murphy began classes in the already built West Hall, and the future University of Portland was established. This event has long been known as the capstone of the first years of Archbishop Christie's term in the archdiocese.

Archbishop Christie also had other projects. A new church, St. Mathew's, was dedicated in Hillsboro, and two new churches, Sacred Heart and St. Michael's Italian National Church, were built in Portland. A series of charitable institutions were also begun in the area—St. Joseph's Home for the Aged, St. Agnes Baby Home, and the House of the Good Shepherd. The Immaculate Conception Church at Stayton was also blessed.

In 1902, the celebration of Archbishop Christie's Silver Jubilee of his ordination to the priesthood was given with great joy in the pro-cathedral. The Bishops of Helena, Montana, and Boise, Idaho, attended along with Bishop O'Dea of Seattle, who preached the sermon. A banquet was held for the visiting bishops and the priests of the archdiocese at Columbia University.

These years of glory and success, however, were followed by a period of trial and conflict. The archbishop saw clearly that eastern Oregon needed to be made into a new diocese. At his suggestion, the Diocese of Baker City was erected, with Father Charles B. O'Reilly as bishop. Bishop O'Reilly had been pastor of Immaculate Heart Parish (old St. Mary's) in Portland, taught in the boys' school in Portland, and had also been editor of the *Catholic Sentinel*. He was a young and active man of considerable general experience. The new bishop was forced from the beginning to use his talents to the utmost as the new diocese had problems almost from the beginning of its existence. One grave problem was the shortage of priests in both the archdiocese of Oregon City and the new Diocese of Baker. As archbishop, Christie had to staff the new diocese with priests from Oregon City. Some of the clergy who had been transferred to Baker were quite resentful.

Thus it was not long before a savage pamphlet appeared, written by an "Unknown Author," attacking Archbishop Christie and supposedly reflecting the sentiments of Bishop O'Reilly and a number of priests of both dioceses as well as some prominent laymen. Copies were circulated widely throughout Portland and other parts of the country, and some even were sent to Rome.

Archbishop Christie decided to avoid making any public statement or reply to this attack. The vicious slander was generally ascribed to a priest named Joseph Schell. Both in the *Catholic Sentinel* and later in the *Oregonian,* strong answers defending Archbishop Christie by priests, sisters, and laymen of the diocese as well as various Catholic societies such as the Knights of Columbus, the Catholic Order of Foresters, and the Cathedral Ladies Aid Society were printed. Archbishop Christie was at this time sick in the hospital as a result of an operation and fatigue due to his heavy schedule. He did not talk about this attack, even around the cathedral.

As he regained his health, Archbishop Christie felt it best to make his "ad lumina" visit to Rome. When he arrived at the Vatican, Pope Pius X (now Saint Pius X) received him with great kindness and presented him with a very handsome ciborium as a personal gift. On the ciborium was engraved the following inscription: "To our venerable brother, Alexander Christie, Archbishop of Oregon City, whose most shining merits on behalf of the Church are right well known to us, we give as a marked testimony of our benevolence this ciborium. From the Vatican Palaces, November 8, 1905, Pius X, Pope."

While in Rome, Archbishop Christie also had an enjoyable visit with Cardinal Merry del Val, the papal secretary of state, with whom he developed a strong personal friendship.

On his return to Portland, Archbishop Christie was met by

a large group of friends and well-wishers who expressed great happiness on behalf of all the Catholic people of the archdiocese that he was once more with them. The crisis had been weathered, and never again during the remaining twenty years of his rule was he to be personally attacked in so vicious a manner.

The archbishop's most pressing problem was the need for new and active priests. There were no local young men available at the moment so the archbishop made every effort to secure priests from outside the Archdiocese of Oregon City. From Minnesota three young men offered their services: George Thompson, his friend Edwin V. O'Hara, and Warren Waite. The three came as students and were ordained as priests of the Archdiocese of Oregon City. Monsignor Charles Smith was secured from the Grand Seminary in Montreal. Others came from Baltimore.

Local candidates were sent to St. Patrick's Seminary in Menlo Park, California, and some even to the North American College in Rome. Archbishop Christie, however, believed that there should be a seminary in the vicinity of Portland. With this in mind, he bought a tract of land along the Willamette River next to the property of the Sisters of the Holy Names. With high hopes of having a thriving seminary, the archbishop persuaded priests from Ireland to staff the seminary, but once they arrived the need for priests was so great that he had no choice but to put them to work in the parishes.

In addition, Archbishop Christie asked religious orders to take parishes in the archdiocese and to supply the clergy to staff them. Thus, the Jesuit Fathers were asked to undertake the parish of St. Ignatius in Portland and the Redemptorist Fathers Holy Redeemer Parish in North Portland. Holy Cross Parish was entrusted to the Holy Cross Fathers who staffed Columbia University, and the Dominican Fathers were asked to build and maintain Holy Rosary Parish. The Benedictine Fathers from Mount Angel undertook Sacred Heart Parish and St. Agatha's Parish. The Servite Fathers undertook a parish in St. Johns.

At this period marking the first ten years of the administration of Archbishop Christie in the Archdiocese of Oregon City,

remarkable growth of the Catholic population (naturally following the growth of Oregon after the Lewis and Clark Exposition
of 1905-1906) was evident. Twenty young men were studying for
the priesthood, and a special appeal was made for the annual
Seminary Fund Collection. In addition to the home for orphaned
and dependent boys so well administered by the Sisters of St.
Mary's of Oregon, meeting the needs of orphan girls was undertaken by the Sisters of the Holy Names. At first a house left
by Father Delorme at St. Paul, Oregon, was used for that purpose.
When the building was burned down, it was replaced by a new
building near the mother house of the sisters. This work continued as Christie Home and was particularly dear to the archbishop's heart. At present, both schools are in operation, but
now largely operated as state institutions funded by state aid.

The archdiocese also supported forty schools enrolling 5,452
pupils taught by 227 teachers. This steady growth continued for
the next ten years until the outbreak of World War I.

During the war, the Catholic people, under the leadership of
Archbishop Christie, participated fully in any and all types of
war work with remarkable success. Despite the shortage of priests,
six were encouraged to go as chaplains—some as regular chaplains and others as chaplains supplied by the Knights of Columbus. (My brother and I were both in the service in those days.)

The horrors of war also included an outbreak of the great
influenza plague. As a result, I was a volunteer orderly, and it was
my job to try to feed those too ill to feed themselves. In room
after room trays were left untouched, except by flies, and out of
our group of two hundred, six or seven died.

When the war was over, Catholics, justifiably proud of their
service and ready response to the calls to serve, thought the
old, anti-Catholic groups in Oregon would forget their bigotry.
This was not to be. In 1920, the local Scottish Rite masons prepared and voted for the Oregon School Bill, which required that
all children between the ages of six and sixteen be sent to public
schools and that failure to do so would render their parents and
guardians subject to fine or imprisonment. Encouraged by this

step, the Ku Klux Klan enrolled many members who were bitterly opposed to Catholics, Jews, and Negroes.

The anti-Catholic groups succeeded in passing the school bill by a shrewd policy of placing their members in strategic positions of government: a majority of members of the school board belonged to one or another of these groups as did all three county commissioners. The Klan had many members in the Portland police force, and there were many cases of violence against those opposed to the church. The "Exalted Cyclops" of the Klan, although not a Catholic himself, was probably the most influential of the anti-Catholic group. His own wife was a Catholic, and his daughters had attended St. Mary's Academy. It is interesting to recall that some years later, after my own ordination, I was privileged to give the last sacraments to his mother-in-law. He himself was present and arranged the Catholic funeral with all courtesy.

The anti-Catholic movement, however, subsided even more rapidly than it had arisen. The school bill was declared unconstitutional by the United States Supreme Court. The legal defense under Judge John P. Kavanaugh and Judge Hall Lusk was backed by the support of Catholics throughout the United States.

The commissioners who had been elected by these persons were caught in an attempt to swindle the people in the building of two new bridges and were recalled. Of all those elected in these years, only the governor survived, and he conveniently forgot to work for the anti-Catholic factions.

Of the Catholic people, their attachment to their faith increased, and many who had not been strong in their faith returned to its practice. In addition, Archbishop Christie formed a Catholic Truth Society which has been of great help indeed. New Catholic schools were built even before the Court decision, and the growth and the prosperity of Catholic schools has been marked.

During this period of stress, Archbishop Christie's spirited defense had strengthened the loyalty of the Catholic people. Although his health had been often tried by serious illness, he continued to labor in the defense of the church. Even though the final decision against the school bill came a few months after his death, he died with the sure knowledge that Catholic education would survive.

Certainly, Archbishop Christie's own courage and kindness to all had deeply endeared him to the church and all its people. More than a century had rendered Alexander Christie one of the greatest of the Archbishops of Portland in Oregon.

5

The Oldest Bishop:
Archbishop Edward D. Howard

Archbishop Edward D. Howard is by far the oldest bishop in the United States and now oldest in the world. At one hundred and two years of age, mere survival is an achievement, but his mind is still clear and his interest in people still great. Even his sense of humor is intact. Contrary to many, closeness of association under his direction gives one even greater regard for him.

I remember vividly his arrival in Portland as the new archbishop. This was in 1926, and I was a seminarian within a year of ordination to the priesthood and hence invited to attend a banquet in his honor. We had been without a bishop for more than a year, and the archdiocese was showing the need of a guiding hand. Since a bishop placed in charge of a diocese is in complete control and bears personal responsibility for the diocese, subject only to the Pope, everyone was most anxious to see what the new archbishop would be like.

He arrived accompanied by his mother, in a good Oregon rain. He was gray-haired, of medium height, and well proportioned. I naturally reasoned that he would doubtless be my superior throughout most of my life as a priest and had a strong personal interest in all that pertained to him.

He had been assigned as a teacher in a college after his own ordination. He was Auxiliary Bishop of Davenport, Iowa, for two years before he came to Portland. As former prefect of discipline in the college it was probable that he would govern the archdiocese well. His reputation was that of a man firm but fair. So coming events cast their shadows before.

As was expected, he began at once to put all in order in the archdiocese. He engaged one of the best accounting firms in Portland to make an adequate survey of the business position of the archdiocese. This at once improved the credit of the administration. There had been no business office, and so he established a chancery office in the front rooms of the cathedral as a temporary expedient. He appointed Father Thomas Tobin as his secretary.

As an educator with many years of experience, he at once began to prepare for a much needed high school for boys in Portland. He began to solicit funds personally in preparation.

In establishing new rules and making new precedents he made it perfectly clear that when a policy was established, it should be followed by all without exception. Years later, when I myself was his secretary, he very clearly remarked to me that he must think matters over very carefully before he made a decision since it must be obeyed.

One of the Irish priests remarked shortly after the archbishop's arrival, "I don't like the set of his jaw. He means business." He did indeed. He was kind and courteous to all and was very approachable. When anyone came to him with a problem, he was easy to talk with but would never permit any rudeness.

His own way of life was simple and unpretentious. He had a strong sense of personal duty and of whatever was proper for a bishop. At first, he moved into the old episcopal residence on Portland Heights, with his mother. He always took at least one long walk each day. His devotion to his mother was deep indeed, and her sudden death was a shock from which he never recovered. He always kept a picture of her on his desk. This was changed at various times to remind him of her various moods so that he was constantly, as it were, in her presence. She never failed to inspire him.

The archbishop's father had been a veteran of the Civil War who had been wounded at the siege of Vicksburg. He recovered from this and marched with Sherman to the sea, but the wound doubtless shortened his life. From his father the archbishop learned to ride and understand horses, and even after he became an archbishop he still enjoyed riding.

After the death of his father, the archbishop's mother took over the family and operated the family stock farm. Although the archbishop was sent to boarding school before he entered the seminary, his mother's strong influence still guided him.

In the summer of 1933, Father Tobin was sent to Rome to take a three-year course in Canon Law, and I was appointed to succeed him as a secretary. This was an office of considerable importance especially since the archbishop was to take a trip around the world and would leave me to represent him. It also made it necessary for me to learn to drive his car for him. He still enjoys reminding me of his various misadventures.

During the archbishop's absence, my duty was to keep him advised of everything of importance and to follow the rules he had laid down with care in the conduct of the diocesan affairs. When he returned, he was very appreciative of all that had been done in his absence. He certainly could not have been kinder or more patient.

Needless to say, I was relieved to have him back and to carry on in the office adjoining his own. By this time, a building had been built, a large part of which was occupied by the chancery office. The archbishop usually walked down to his office and was so punctual that one could set his watch by the time of his arrival.

After a busy morning during which callers had been introduced to him and varied affairs of the archdiocese were transacted, we usually went out to luncheon together. This was followed by calls on any sick priests in the hospitals after which he returned to his own residence.

I had a very intimate relationship with the archbishop and came to see a different side of church administration. Often hard and perplexing problems arose, and at several times real difficulties had to be placed before the archbishop. Yet I did not see him worried or excited. He met everything with courage and wisdom. Even when there had been disloyalty toward him, he was very careful to avoid any unfairness even toward any with whom he had every reason to be displeased. He did not put off important decisions but grappled with each problem as it arose.

Upon the return of Father Tobin from Rome, he resumed his position in the chancery office and I returned to ordinary parochial work. Although I no longer had the close association with the archbishop, he remained the same kindly and understanding superior. One could always call upon him and discuss matters with the utmost frankness. Looking back over the long vista of the years, I can certainly say that I never talked matters over without emerging with a greater admiration for him.

Many years have passed. The archdiocese has grown and prospered under his long administration. When the Second Vatican Council was assembled in 1963, Archbishop Howard attended the first session and was introduced to Pope John XXIII as the oldest archbishop in the Uniited States. Afterward he secured permission to stay away from the remaining sessions. But he kept in careful touch with all that went on. All policies determined were accepted by him with the utmost loyalty.

When it was decided that pastors, bishops, and even cardinals should retire at the age of seventy-five, the archbishop, who had long passed that age, at once sent in his resignation. But his heart has remained with the priests and the people of the Archdiocese of Portland in Oregon, and he realized how much all longed to have him remain with them. He is now settled down in a pleasant residence near the mother house of the Sisters of St. Mary's of Oregon. He is still particularly close to all and is an inspiration to everyone. He is particularly happy to have the priests call upon him and talk over the past and the present. His sense of humor sparkles, and his loyalty to God and the church is very evident. He attends church celebrations and funerals with unfailing respect.

Fifty fertile years among us have borne lasting fruit. When called upon, he can still give a ringing and uplifting talk. His love and respect for priests and people are evident.

6

Most Reverend Robert Joseph Dwyer: Second Bishop of Reno, Sixth Archbishop of Portland in Oregon

By Brother Gerard Brassard, A.A., in the *Encyclopedia of the Catholic Bishops of America.*

ROBERT JOSEPH DWYER—Born, August 1, 1908, Salt Lake City, Utah, the son of John Charles and Mabel Maynard Dwyer. He attended the public schools of his native city; Judge Memorial High School, Salt Lake City; St. Mary Manor, South Langhorne, Pennsylvania; St. Patrick's Seminary, Menlo Park, California; postgraduate studies at The Catholic University of America, Washington D.C., 1938-1941. He was ordained June 11, 1932, Salt Lake City, Utah, by Bishop Edward J. Kelly of Boise. He was the first native ordained for the diocesan clergy. Engaged in pastoral work in the Diocese of Salt Lake City: Assistant at the Cathedral of the Madeleine, Salt Lake City, 1932-1934; Vice Rector in 1947 and Rector of the Cathedral of the Madeleine, Salt Lake City, 1948-1952; Chaplain and Instructor of the College of St. Mary of the Wabash, Salt Lake City, 1934-1938; Chaplain of the Newman Club of the University of Utah, 1933-1938; Editor and Business Manager of the *Intermountain Catholic* and its successor, the *Intermountain*

36

Catholic Edition of The Register (official paper of the diocese), 1938, 1942-1946, 1950-1952. Superintendent of Schools in the Diocese of Salt Lake City, 1941; Diocesan Director of the Society for the Propagation of the Faith; Promoter of Justice in the diocesan tribunal. He is the author of several historical works on Utah and one of the most outstanding Catholic editorial writers of the nation. Named a papal Chamberlain in 1950.

Elected by Pope Pius XII to the See of Reno, May 19, 1952. He was consecrated August 5, 1952, Cathedral of the Madeleine, Salt Lake City, Utah, by Archbishop John J. Mitty of San Francisco, assisted by Bishop Thomas K. Gorman, Coadjutor Bishop of Dallas, and Bishop Gorman transferred to the coadjutorship of Dallas. He convened the First Synod for the priests of the Diocese of Reno, September 27, 1957. He attended the Second Vatican Council, 1962-1965. A member of the administrative committee of the National Conference of Catholic Bishops, Washington, D.C., November 1966.

Promoted by Pope Paul VI to the Metropolitan See of Portland in Oregon, December 9, 1966. He was installed, Cathedral of the Immaculate Conception, Portland, Oregon, February 6, 1967, succeeding Archbishop Edward D. Howard, who resigned. He received the sacred Pallium from the hands of his predecessor Archbishop Edward D. Howard, November 23, 1967. Chairman of the editorial board of a Catholic weekly magazine, *Twin Circle—The National Catholic Press,* September 1967.

BLAZON—Impaled Dexter: Per fess azure and argent, on a fess wavy gules three mullets of six points of the second, in chief a crescent of the first (See of Portland in Oregon); *Sinister: Argent: A lion rampant gules between three ermine spots sable, two in chief and one in base* (Dwyer). MOTTO: *Levate oculos vestros.* "Lift up your eyes." (John 4:35). SIGNIFICANCE—In the dexter impalement are the arms of the Archdiocese explained on page. . . . The sinister impalement are the arms of the Archbishop who uses the shield of the Irish O'Dwyer family.

The motto is taken from the Gospel of St. John Apostle and Evangelist, chapter 4, verse 35. The complete verse reads: *Nonne vos dicitis quod adhuc quatuor menses sunt, et messis venit? Ecce dico vobis: Levate oculos vestros et videte regiones, quia albae sunt jam ad messam,* which is translated: "Do you not say: 'There are yet four months and then comes the harvest?' Well I say to you, lift up your eyes and behold that the fields are already white for the harvest." A motto briefly expresses an ideal, a program of life, and the spirit of the one who selects it.

7

The Return of Archbishop Dwyer

After the retirement of Archbishop Howard, the Most Reverend Robert J. Dwyer, Bishop of Reno, Nevada, was appointed his successor. This was on December 14, 1966. I was flown to Reno as one of the diocesan consultors to bring our new archbishop to Portland. He received us with great courtesy and returned to Portland with us. He was evidently a man of ability. After the round of ceremonies, he began at once to adjust to the new responsibilities. Getting to know priests and people with all their problems was indeed a task. There were, of course, the old conservatives and the young radicals, as could be expected. There were vexations and trials which could be inevitable. Following Cardinal Newman's concept of a gentleman, Archbishop Dwyer hated to cause pain to any person and tried to get someone else to break the news of transfers and appointments which he knew to be necessary. As a man of great sensitivity himself, this bothered him. The ceremonies of the mass and of the liturgy of the church were carried out by him with care and great love.

He secured a new residence where he always showed himself as a charming host. One could never appreciate him unless he could be seen in the environment he had created. Attacks and criticism he felt deeply, but he tried to avoid public controversy. He surrounded himself with a splendid library which he used constantly.

As a man of great literary ability, he continued to write for the press in his own inimitable way. Humor and learning showed forth in every line of his many articles. When one could see him in his own home environment, at the altar of his own chapel, or in his library, one naturally admired and respected him.

But the world of the sixties and seventies has been a very difficult and hard one. Controversies of all kinds arose. In his own sermons and writings he fought valiantly for the church and her laws and her liturgy. He did not and could not sacrifice the things he believed to be just and right just to avoid the attacks against them both within and without the church. But this brought strain and pain to a man who was not physically strong. There was a heart weakness which he well knew to be very dangerous, although he concealed this and did not permit it to be advertised. It is not necessary or proper to go into these matters here, but they were very real. In addition to this, there were many difficult administrative problems, all of which brought on strain.

Finally, there came a great and savage controversy regarding certain schoolteaching directives which he was sure were dangerous. Here he felt it necessary to order certain personnel changes which subjected him to violent public attacks. His position was much misunderstood, and a good deal of disloyalty was shown where he felt he should have had loyal support.

The strain of this brought about two serious heart attacks which he realized might at some time result in his death. The possibility of a long interregnum during which the interests of the church in Oregon might suffer caused him to make a difficult decision. He wrote to the Pope advising of the difficulties of his health and submitting his resignation. This must have caused regret in Rome, but it was accepted and a new appointment made.

Archbishop Dwyer purchased a new home in Piedmont, California, and moved his chapel, library, and furniture to it. He then arranged literary and other important responsibilities to be carried on from there. There was no question of his fondness for Portland and his hope eventually to return to it. We were happy, indeed, to hear from him and to know that he had not forgotten us. But the grave dangers to his health increased, and we learned with sorrow that his death was to be expected at almost any time.

He himself was quite aware of this, and his courage and faith were a source of admiration to all who came in contact with him. He died on March 24, 1976. We learned with happiness that he had wishes to be returned to Portland and be buried among us.

Archbishop Power, his successor in Portland, kept priests and people informed and arranged the funeral from the cathedral. There was never a more inspiring ceremony than this. During the Sunday before the funeral, large numbers of priests, sisters, and people visited the cathedral to pray for him, and the office for the dead was arranged in the late afternoon.

On March 29, a requiem mass was celebrated in the cathedral. The celebrated mass was offered up with Archbishop Power presiding and joined by twelve bishops and three hundred priests. The music was sung by a choir of priests. Cardinal Timothy Manning, of Los Angeles, California, preached a moving homily in which he recalled the deep and passionate love of the mass which was so characteristic of Archbishop Dwyer. The archbishop had preached the sermon at the first mass of Cardinal Manning himself as his personal friend. That same love of the mass, and all that was connected with it, had always shown itself through the life of the archbishop.

At the close of the mass a telegram from the Vatican was read as follows:

> The Holy Father prays for the soul of Archbishop Robert Dwyer, invoking upon him peace and joy in the Risen Christ. To the Archdiocese of Portland as it mourns its former pastor, with Christian hope, His Holiness imparts an Apostolic Blessing.

The predecessor of Archbishop Dwyer, Archbishop Howard, issued the following statement: "He was greatly gifted especially in a literary way, and accomplished a tremendous amount of good."

Some seventy-two cars joined the procession to Mt. Calvary Cemetery for the vault entombment. There the coffin was blessed and sprinkled with holy water by Archbishop Power and many priests.

It was with deep feeling indeed that the body of the deceased archbishop was received and left as he had requested in his former archdiocese where every mark of affection and regret was manifested toward one who had served it so well.

8

Archbishop Cornelius M. Power

The seventh Archbishop of Portland in Oregon was peculiarly fitted to carry on the work of that important see. He was carefully prepared by his studies and experience for that appointment. He was the son of a most devout family. His father and mother were deeply pious, and from the same family two sisters were attached to the Sisters of the Holy Names and were dedicated to the work of Christian education. His father was William Power and his mother Kate Dougherty. In his educational preparation, every effort was made to render his priestly life of the greatest value in the priesthood. While his earliest life was in the public school, he passed on to the parochial school and later to the O'Dea High School, from which he went on to St. Joseph's in Mountain View, California, for preparatory seminary. Afterward he went on to St. Patrick's Major Seminary in Menlo Park, California, for two years. The remaining two years were spent in St. Edward's Seminary in Kenmore, Washington. Realizing the need in the diocese for higher studies in Canon Law, he passed on to the Catholic University of America School of Canon Law in Washington, D.C. From this he obtained a Doctorate in Canon Law. At the time of his graduation from the seminary he had been ordained to the priesthood in Seattle by Archbishop Gerald Shaughonessy. After his reception of his Doctorate in Canon Law, he returned to Seattle, where he served in a large number of assignments in Seattle and in the chancery office. He was made first administrator and then a pastor of the parish of Our Lady of the Lake. During this period, he was used frequently for many different causes and was made Chancellor of the Archdiocese of Seattle. Appointed a domestic prelate on January 12, 1963, it was not surprising that, when the new Archdiocese of Yakima had gotten into serious troubles, he was appointed the second archbishop of that see. I recall vividly that when I congratulated him on that appointment he remarked that it probably was not a subject for congratulations. In any event, he worked very successfully in that capacity and was much beloved by priests and people.

After the resignation of Archbishop Dwyer, he was made the seventh Archbishop of Portland in Oregon on January 22, 1974. Although he was not well himself, he made a point of visiting Archbishop Howard, who had retired as archbishop and was living in a home supplied by the Sisters of St. Mary's of Oregon. Later he himself was in the hospital as a patient. There a doctor performed a painful operation from which he recovered without any serious difficulties. After this and for some time he lived in the guest quarters of the Convent of the Angels of the Sisters of St. Francis of Philadelphia on Palatine Hill in Portland, Oregon. Eventually, he took an unfinished convent adjacent to the La Salle Campus, which he had finished with a chapel, dining and living room, and parlor, four bedrooms, a kitchen, and a housekeeper's quarters. He was working from there to visit the parishes of the archdiocese and to go to the chancery office regularly.

Archbishop Power came to the conclusion that he was in need of help to assist in the work of the church and accordingly asked for such help. After long and careful consideration it was evident that this was important for the church. Two auxiliary bishops were accordingly appointed and consecrated. They are the Most Reverend Paul E. Waldschmidt, C.S.C., who had long served to be in charge of the University of Portland, and the Most Reverend Kenneth D. Steiner, D.D. Both have become important helpers to Archbishop Power.